BROWN v. BOARD OF EDUCATION

A DAY THAT CHANGED AMERICA

by Margeaux Weston

CAPSTONE PRESS
a capstone imprint

Capstone Captivate is published by Capstone Press, an imprint of Capstone.
1710 Roe Crest Drive, North Mankato, Minnesota 56003
www.capstonepub.com

Library of Congress Cataloging-in-Publication Data
Names: Weston, Margeaux, author.
Title: Brown v. Board of Education : a day that changed America / by Margeaux Weston.
Other titles: Brown versus Board of Education
Description: North Mankato : Capstone Press, 2022. | Series: Days that changed America | Includes bibliographical references and index. | Audience: Ages 8-11 | Audience: Grades 4-6 | Summary: "On May 17, 1954, the Supreme Court of the United States delivered a unanimous ruling that declared racial segregation in public schools was unconstitutional, because separate could never be equal. Now readers can step back in time to learn about what led up to this major milestone in the Civil Rights movement, how the landmark case unfolded, and the ways in which one critical day changed America forever"-- Provided by publisher.
Identifiers: LCCN 2021012614 (print) | LCCN 2021012615 (ebook) | ISBN 9781663920577 (paperback) | ISBN 9781663905710 (hardcover) | ISBN 9781663905680 (pdf) | ISBN 9781663905703 (kindle edition)
Subjects: LCSH: Brown, Oliver, 1918-1961--Trials, litigation, etc.--Juvenile literature. | Topeka (Kan.). Board of Education--Trials, litigation, etc.--Juvenile literature. | Segregation in education--Law and legislation--United States--Juvenile literature. | Discrimination in education--Law and legislation--United States--Juvenile literature. | African Americans--Civil rights--Juvenile literature.
Classification: LCC KF228.B76 W47 2022 (print) | LCC KF228.B76 (ebook) | DDC 344.73/0798--dc23
LC record available at https://lccn.loc.gov/2021012614
LC ebook record available at https://lccn.loc.gov/2021012615

Image Credits
Associated Press: 7, 18, 22, 23, 24, North Wind Picture Archives, 9; Collection of the Smithsonian National Museum of African American History and Culture, Gift of Kate Clark Harris in memory of her parents Kenneth and Mamie Clark, in cooperation with the Northside Center for Child Development: 19; Getty Images: Corbis/Joseph Schwartz, 6, The LIFE Images Collection/Carl Iwasaki, 14, 15, The LIFE Images Collection/Don Cravens, 26, The LIFE Picture Collection/Robert W. Kelley, 17; Library of Congress: cover, 5, 12, 21, 25; National Archives and Records Administration: 10; Newscom: Everett Collection, 20; Shutterstock: Atoly (design element), cover and throughout, Cameron Whitman, 11, Everett Collection, 8, mark reinstein, 27, Michael Scott Milner, 13

Editorial Credits
Editor: Abby Huff; Media Researcher: Svetlana Zhurkin; Production Specialist: Laura Manthe

Consultant Credits
Dr. W. Marvin Dulaney, Associate Professor of History Emeritus, University of Texas, Arlington

All internet sites appearing in back matter were available and accurate when this book was sent to press.

TABLE OF CONTENTS

Words in **bold** are in the glossary.

On May 17, 1954, the American people waited to hear a ruling from the Supreme Court. The nine **justices** decided whether **segregation** in schools was legal. Across the South, state laws kept white and Black students apart. The justices reviewed five cases that challenged those laws. Together, the cases were known as *Brown v. Board of Education*. Now, the justices had made a decision. All nine agreed. It was wrong to have separate schools based on skin color.

The nation's response was split. Many white people in the South were mad. Other people in the nation thought it was the right thing to do. But, in a time when Black people were protesting for **civil rights**, it showed change was coming. The Supreme Court's ruling would be one of the first steps toward equality in the United States.

After the Supreme Court's decision, lawyers (left to right) George E. C. Hayes, Thurgood Marshall, and James M. Nabrit Jr. celebrated on the steps outside the court building.

CHAPTER 1

SEPARATE WORLDS

Before 1954, each state had its own laws about segregation. In some northern states, all children went to school together. But in southern states, Black and white students could not go to the same schools.

Not all schools kept students apart. In 1940s Brooklyn, New York, Black and white students walked home together after school.

The separate schools were supposed to be equal. But often, schools for Black children were not as good. Some schools did not have running water or electricity. Other schools were overcrowded or only had one classroom. Sometimes textbooks were damaged or missing pages. The segregated schools were not equal.

A rural, two-room schoolhouse for Black students in 1950

Segregation came from a long history of treating Black people poorly. In 1565, the first **enslaved** Africans were brought to America. Enslaved people had no rights. They were treated like property. They were often beaten. Many did heavy work on large farms called plantations. Slavery in America did not end until after the Civil War in 1865.

In the 1600s, enslaved Africans were brought to all the American colonies, but many ended up in the South to work on farms.

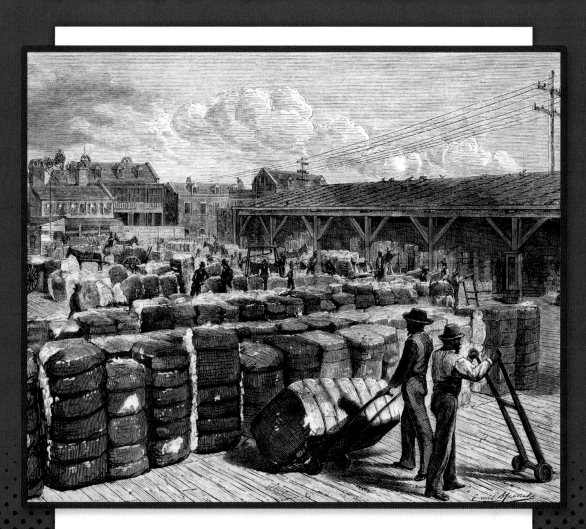

Black dock workers unloaded cotton in Charleston, South Carolina, in the 1870s.

Black people were now free. But they were still not treated fairly. Laws stopped them from getting good jobs. They could not own land. In 1868, Congress passed the Fourteenth Amendment. This gave all people born in the U.S. equal rights. It made it against the law for states to treat people unequally. But southern states did not follow the rules.

Starting in late 1870s, states in the South created their own laws. These laws kept Black and white people apart. They were called **Jim Crow laws**. The laws applied to schools and many areas of daily life. They were meant to **oppress** Black people.

Homer Plessy challenged the laws in New Orleans. He tried to board a train car for whites only. Police arrested him. Plessy later took his case to the Supreme Court. In 1896, the justices ruled that it was legal to separate people based on race, as long as the spaces were equal. This set up the "separate but equal" idea. It made it legal for Black people to be treated unfairly. The court's decision led to more Jim Crow laws.

The Supreme Court's ruling in the *Plessy v. Ferguson* case let states create more unfair segregation laws.

THE U.S. SUPREME COURT

The U.S. Supreme Court is the highest court in the nation. Members of the Supreme Court are called justices. The president chooses the justices. Then the person must be confirmed by the U.S. Senate. The Supreme Court decides whether laws or actions are allowed by the U.S. Constitution. Their decisions affect many people because state courts use their rulings to decide on similar cases. Supreme Court justices are trusted to make fair decisions.

The Supreme Court Building in Washington, D.C.

CHAPTER 2

BROWN V. BOARD

Many people were fighting for fair treatment. One group was the National Association for the Advancement of Colored People (NAACP). This civil rights group formed in 1909. It raised money to go to court to fight for equality.

As a lawyer, Thurgood Marshall worked on many cases that fought for civil rights.

In 1940, Thurgood Marshall was a lawyer. He was also a leader in the NAACP. Marshall and his team argued that segregation went against the Fourteenth Amendment. They knew that separate was not equal. Marshall wanted to prove once and for all that separation based on skin color was **unconstitutional**. He decided to first focus on laws related to education.

SOMETHING WORTH FIGHTING FOR

The NAACP is one of America's oldest and largest civil rights organizations. It was formed by white and Black people. The group fought against the violence Black people were experiencing across the nation. It supported laws to protect Black people. It also won many court cases that helped Black people gain more freedom. Today, the NAACP has about 500,000 members worldwide. It still works to make sure all people have equal rights.

People marching in a rally organized by the NAACP in Atlanta, Georgia, in 2020

In 1951, Linda Brown had to walk six blocks to catch a school bus to the Black school she attended. She was only in third grade. Her father, Oliver Brown, wanted to enroll her in the closer white school. The school board denied the request. It also denied 12 other Black families. The NAACP took the families' cases to court to fight segregation. The case was named *Oliver Brown et al. v. The Board of Education of Topeka, Kansas.*

Linda Brown was not allowed to go to the school near her home because of segregation laws.

Oliver Brown (back row, second from left) and the other families did not give up when their case lost at the state level.

The state court ruled against the Black students. This did not stop Marshall. The NAACP and Marshall prepared to bring the case to the Supreme Court. The court had the power to make the final decision. The NAACP hoped that the court would **reverse** the "separate but equal" decision from 1896 and finally **integrate** schools.

CHAPTER 3

BRINGING EVERYONE TOGETHER

A year had passed since the first *Brown v. Board* case was heard in Kansas. The NAACP had also presented four other cases involving elementary schools across the nation. The U.S. Supreme Court finally agreed to hear all five cases at once. Marshall now had the chance to argue for the end of school segregation.

On December 9, 1952, Marshall and the NAACP lawyers started to present the case to the Supreme Court. They had to show that separate but equal laws were not fair. They showed how Black schools were given fewer resources. In one case, Black students had to crowd into a one-room shack for school. White students had a proper building. But Marshall knew he had to show more. He had to prove the very act of segregation was wrong.

Some of the cases in *Brown v. Board* showed how Black students did not have equal school buildings and supplies.

The work of Dr. Kenneth Clark and more than 30 other expert researchers was used to show how segregation was harmful to children.

Marshall argued that separating students by skin color was harmful to Black children. Even with the same type of building or supplies, the Black students were not being treated equally.

FACT

In the 1940s, toy companies did not make Black dolls. The researchers had to paint white dolls brown in order for the Black children to see dolls that looked like them.

To show this, Marshall asked expert researchers to present their work. Kenneth and Mamie Clark had tested Black children across the nation. The children were given a choice between a Black doll and a white doll. The children mostly chose white dolls. They did not like the Black dolls. The researchers said that this showed segregation caused Black children to feel bad about themselves.

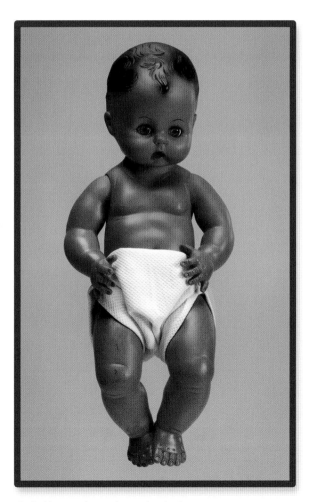

A painted doll used in the Clarks' tests

The justices listened to Marshall's team, but they could not agree. They wanted more information. In 1953, they asked both teams to come back to present their cases again.

FACT

One of the Supreme Court justices died before *Brown v. Board* was decided. He was replaced by Earl Warren. Warren worked to make sure all the justices agreed on a ruling.

Marshall (center) and the other NAACP lawyers worked to be ready to argue their case for a second time.

Crowds of people lined up outside of the court building. They wanted to get a seat inside to hear the arguments. The Supreme Court's ruling would be important. It would show whether the U.S. government still supported treating Black people unfairly.

The lines outside the Supreme Court on December 7, 1953

Months later, the Supreme Court reached a decision. On May 17, 1954, all nine justices ruled that segregated public schools were unlawful. They agreed with Marshall that separate schools could never be equal. This ruling made segregation in education unconstitutional. Public schools would finally have to integrate.

FACT

In 1967, Thurgood Marshall became the first African American to be appointed to the Supreme Court.

The U.S. Supreme Court justices who decided *Brown v. Board*

In September 1954, students at an integrated school in Washington, D.C., rushed outside for recess.

The Supreme Court's ruling said schools must integrate. But it did not say when. Many southern states ignored the order. The Supreme Court gave a new ruling in 1955. It said that integration had to happen "with all **deliberate** speed." But this ruling did not set a deadline either.

CHAPTER 4

SLOW ROAD TO EQUALITY

The Supreme Court's decision ended segregation laws in public schools. But southern states did not follow the order for many years. People in the South were used to having everything separate. Many white people did not want change.

Many years after *Brown v. Board*, white families still protested against integrated schools.

In 1957, President Eisenhower sent armed troops. They protected Black students integrating a white high school in Little Rock, Arkansas. White people had gathered to shout and throw things at the Black students. They stopped the students from entering the school.

In Alabama, schools stayed segregated. In 1963, the governor of Alabama blocked the doors for two Black students who wanted to enroll at the University of Alabama. Years had passed since *Brown v. Board*, but it was clear that change would not happen easily.

Armed troops walked with Black students in Little Rock as they left school to keep them safe from angry white crowds.

Despite the challenges, *Brown v. Board* was a major win for civil rights. The Supreme Court's ruling had set up the idea that it was wrong to keep people apart based on skin color. It led the way for getting rid of segregation in every area of life.

After a lot of hard work, Black people started to get more rights. One of the first victories was the Civil Rights Act of 1957. This law made it illegal to keep Black people from voting. In 1964, Congress passed a new Civil Rights Act. It made segregation in all areas illegal. It made **discrimination** illegal too. The law said people could not be treated unfairly because of their race, color, religion, gender, or where they were born. Jim Crow laws were finally ending.

In 1957, Black passengers got on a newly integrated bus after more than a year of fighting for an end to separate seating.

Monroe Elementary, the segregated school Linda Brown attended, is now a National Historic Site.

The *Brown v. Board* decision protected the right to an equal education. It also led the way for civil rights for all people. Almost 70 years later, it is still a historic case that forever changed America.

TIMELINE

DECEMBER 6, 1865: The Thirteenth Amendment is put into law and ends slavery in America.

JULY 9, 1868: The Fourteenth Amendment gives Black people equal protection under the law.

LATE 1870S: Southern states begin creating Jim Crow laws that treat Black people unfairly and segregate all areas of life.

MAY 18, 1896: The Supreme Court rules on the case *Plessy v. Ferguson.* It says segregation based on race is lawful and sets up the "separate but equal" idea.

FEBRUARY 12, 1909: The NAACP forms to help protect Black people from the violence and injustice happening across the nation.

AUGUST 3, 1951: In *Oliver Brown et al. v. The Board of Education of Topeka, Kansas,* the state court decides that "separate but equal" is lawful.

DECEMBER 9, 1952: Thurgood Marshall and the NAACP bring *Brown v. Board* to the Supreme Court, along with four other cases. The court cannot come to a decision.

DECEMBER 7, 1953: The Supreme Court listens to the second round of arguments in *Brown v. Board.*

MAY 17, 1954: The Supreme Court rules on *Brown v. Board*. All nine justices agree segregation in public schools is unconstitutional.

MAY 31, 1955: The Supreme Court rules on *Brown II* and says that schools must desegregate "with all deliberate speed."

SEPTEMBER 4, 1957: Nine Black students integrating a high school in Little Rock, Arkansas, are met with violence and are not allowed to come in.

SEPTEMBER 9, 1957: The Civil Rights Act of 1957 passes, making it illegal to deny a citizen's right to vote.

JULY 2, 1964: The Civil Rights Act of 1964 passes, making segregation and discrimination illegal.

GLOSSARY

civil rights (SIH-vuhl RAYTS)—the rights that all people have to freedom and equal treatment under the law

deliberate (dih-LIB-uh-ruht)—done on purpose or in a way that is planned

discrimination (dih-skrih-muh-NAY-shuhn)—the act of treating people unfairly because of their race, country of birth, gender, or another difference

enslaved (en-SLAYVD)—a person who is the property of another and is forced to work for free, without any pay

integrate (IN-tuh-grayt)—to bring different groups together as equals

Jim Crow laws (JIM KROH LAWZ)—state or local laws in the South that enforced segregation, requiring Black and white people to be kept apart

justice (JUH-stihss)—a judge in a court of law, especially the highest court

oppress (oh-PRESS)—to treat someone in a cruel, unjust, and hard way

reverse (ri-VURSS)—opposite in position, order, or direction

segregation (seh-gruh-GAY-shuhn)—the act of separating a group of people by their race or culture

unconstitutional (uhn-kon-stih-TOO-shuh-nul)—something that is unlawful based on the rules of the U.S. Constitution

READ MORE

Magoon, Kekla. *The Highest Tribute: Thurgood Marshall's Life, Leadership, and Legacy.* New York: Quill Tree Books, 2021.

Raum, Elizabeth. *The Life of Ruby Bridges.* Mankato, MN: Amicus Ink, 2019.

Smith, Sherri L. *What Is the Civil Rights Movement?* New York: Penguin Workshop, 2020

INTERNET SITES

National Geographic Kids: Thurgood Marshall
kids.nationalgeographic.com/history/article/thurgood-marshall

Smithsonian National Museum of American History: Separate Is Not Equal
americanhistory.si.edu/brown/history/index.html

TIME for Kids: Civil Rights
timeforkids.com/g34/g3-text-set-civilrights/

INDEX